SUPER SiLLY,
AWESOMELY HiLARiOUS,
FUNNY BONE-TICKLING

JOKES
for Kids

999 SUPER SILLY, AWESOMELY HILARIOUS, FUNNY BONE-TICKLING JOKES for Kids

Jodi and Lilly Simmons
with JoAnne Simmons

BARBOUR BOOKS
An Imprint of Barbour Publishing, Inc.

Published by Barbour Books, an imprint of Barbour Publishing, Inc., 1810 Barbour Drive, Uhrichsville, Ohio 44683, www.barbourbooks.com

Our mission is to inspire the world with the life-changing message of the Bible.

Member of the
Evangelical Christian
Publishers Association

Printed in the United States of America.
06063   0418   OP

CONTENTS

. . . .

INTRODUCTION

Hi, everybody! We're Jodi and Lilly Simmons. We're sisters; we're ten and eight years old, and we LOVE to LAUGH!

That's why we wanted to put together a big collection of all of our favorite jokes to share with other kids. Some of these jokes may make you giggle. Others might make you fall on the floor and laugh. . .and *some* of them may even make you roll your eyes. (Those are the kinds of jokes our mom and dad tell.)

Jokes are fun to read to yourself, but they're even *better* to read out loud. So share all of these 999 jokes with friends, family, teachers—anybody who will listen!

Jodi and Lilly

ANIMAL ANTICS

1. How do you catch a rabbit?
   Hide in the bushes and sound like a carrot.

2. What is a bird's favorite food?
   Chocolate chirp cookies.

3. Why do porcupines never lose games?
   Because they always have more points than any other animal.

4. What did the parrot say on Independence Day?
   "Polly wants a firecracker."

5. What keys are found in the animal kingdom?

Donkeys, monkeys, and turkeys.

6. Where do elephants pack their vacation clothes?

In their trunks.

7. Why did the panda eat bamboo?

He wanted a green thumb.

8. How do elephants communicate?

With elephones.

9. How do you make an elephant float?

Get root beer. Pour it over vanilla ice cream. Add an elephant.

10. How do you save a hippopot-amus drowning in hot cocoa?
  Throw it a marshmallow.

11. Why does the giraffe have such a long neck?
  So it won't have to smell its feet.

12. What kind of turtle always has a bad attitude?
  A snapping turtle.

13. Where do wasps live?
  Stingapore.

14. What kind of pictures do turtles take?
  Shell-fies.

15. What do penguins like to eat best?
   Brrr-itos.

16. Why did the manager hire the marsupial?
   It was koala-fied.

17. Who comes to a picnic but is never invited?
   Ants.

18. What do you get when you cross an alligator with a pickle?
   A croco-dill.

19. Where do cows ride rollercoasters?
   At a-moo-sement parks.

20. What hops around holding up banks?
   A robbit.

21. How did the lion greet the zebras?
   "Pleased to eat you."

22. What did one fox say to another?
   "I'm tired of being hounded all the time."

23. What do you call mouse shoes?
   Squeakers.

24. What do you call flying monkeys?
   Hot-air baboons.

25. Why did the otter cross the road?
    To get to the otter side.

26. What do mice do all day at home?
    Mousework.

27. How do mice keep their breath fresh all day long?
    They rinse with mousewash.

28. What did Mr. Bee say to Mrs. Bee when he got home from work?
    "Hi, honey!"

29. Why did the queen bee kick out all the other bees?
    Because they kept droning on and on.

30. How did the chimpanzee break out of its cage?
    With a monkey wrench.

31. What does a bee do when it's too hot?
    He takes off his yellow jacket.

32. What's the happiest animal in the wild?
    The happy-potamus.

33. What do little mice love to play with their friends?
    Hide-and-squeak.

34. What is the rudest type of bird?
    The mockingbird.

35. Why is it hard to talk to a ram?
He keeps butting in.

36. How do monkeys get down the stairs?
They slide down the banana-ster.

37. How do fireflies start a race?
"Ready! Set! Glow!"

38. What do marsupials love to drink?
Koka-Koala.

39. How do you know when you're dealing with a tough mosquito?
When you slap it, it slaps you back!

40. What kind of rabbits are good at fixing flat tires?
   Jackrabbits.

41. What's black and white, black and white, black and white?
   A panda bear rolling down the mountain.

42. What's black and white, black and white, black and white, black and white, black and white, black and white?
   A panda bear and a zebra rolling down the mountain.

43. What's black and white, black and white, black and white—and stinky?
   A skunk rolling down the mountain.

44. How did the slug say good-bye to his friend?

"See you next slime!"

45. Why does a bear sleep three months out of the year?

No one is brave enough to wake it up.

46. Why did the bird go to the doctor?

He needed medical tweet-ment.

47. Who did the parakeet marry?

His high school tweet-heart.

48. Where do you treat an injured wasp?

At the waspital.

49. What did the elephants wear at the swimming pool?
Trunks.

50. What kind of bee is so hard to understand?
A mumble-bee.

51. What kind of shoes do frogs wear?
Open-toad slippers.

52. What do you call a nine-foot-high stack of frogs?
A toadem pole.

53. What kinds of movies do frogs like best?
The ones with hoppy endings.

54. What do you call an elephant that never takes a bath?
   A smell-ephant.

55. Where do birds invest their money?
   In the stork market.

56. What's a firefly's favorite game?
   Hide-and-glow-seek.

57. What do bees like to chew?
   Buzzlegum.

58. What kind of insects live on the moon?
   Lunar-ticks.

59. Why was the squirrel late for work?
Because traffic was nuts.

60. What kind of insect marries a ladybug?
A gentlemanbug.

61. Where do spiders check their spelling?
Webster's Dictionary.

62. What's a parrot's favorite game?
Hide-and-speak.

63. How do spiders prefer their corn?
On the cobweb.

64. How do snails fight?
They slug it out.

65. What kind of flower do frogs like the best?
Croakuses.

66. What's the tallest flower in the world?
The giraffodil.

67. What kind of insects love a good tune?
Humbugs.

68. Why do bees hum?
Because they can't remember the words.

69. What animal should you never play a board game with?
    A cheetah.

70. What composer do bugs love best?
    Bee-thoven.

71. What happened after Mr. and Mrs. Snake argued?
    They hissed and made up.

72. What do you get if you cross a snowman with an alligator?
    Frostbite.

73. What do you get if you cross a kangaroo and an iguana?
    Leaping lizards.

74. What do you get when you cross a pig and a centipede?
Bacon and legs.

75. Why are gophers so busy?
They always have to gopher this and gopher that.

76. What did the mother buffalo say to her boy as he was leaving?
"Bison."

77. How does a beaver know which tree to cut down?
Whichever one he chews.

78. Why was the baby ant confused?
Because all his uncles were ants.

79. Where do polar bears like to vacation?
   Brrr-muda.

80. What's a penguin's favorite sandwich?
   A cheese brrrr-ger.

81. What kind of bee is clumsy and drops everything?
   A fumblebee.

82. What do you call a grizzly bear with no teeth?
   A gummy bear.

83. How do bears walk around?
   With bear feet.

84. How does a bee get to school?
It takes the buzz.

85. What did the bee say to his friend the flower?
"You are my best bud."

86. What did the bee say to his barber?
"Just give me a buzz."

87. What do you call a new bee?
A babe-bee.

88. What kind of bee has a hard time making up its mind?
A may-bee.

89. How do baby birds learn to fly?
   They wing it.

90. What kind of dance do woodpeckers excel at?
   Tap dance.

91. What bird can lift the most?
   A crane.

92. Which bird is always out of breath?
   A puffin.

93. What happened when the lion ate the comedian?
   He felt funny.

94. What do you get if you cross a parrot with a shark?
A bird that will talk your ear off.

95. What Christmas carol do monkeys love best?
"Jungle Bells."

96. How do chickens stay fit?
With regular eggs-ercise.

97. How does a bunny style his fur?
With hare spray.

98. What vegetable do you get when an elephant walks through your garden?
Squash!

99. How do you know if an elephant plans to stay the weekend?
See if he brought his trunk.

100. Why did they throw the elephants out of the swimming pool?
Because they couldn't keep their trunks up.

101. What is a bonobo's favorite cookie?
Chocolate chimp.

102. What time is it when an elephant sits on your fence?
Time to get a new fence.

103. What is as big as an elephant but doesn't weigh an ounce?
An elephant's shadow.

104. What kind of automobile does an elephant drive?
One with plenty of trunk space.

105. What are goose bumps for?
To keep geese from speeding.

106. What's the best way to send a letter to a bunny?
By hare mail.

107. What do you call a bear when he's out in the rain?
A drizzly bear.

108. Where does a skunk sit in church?
In a pew.

109. What do you get if you cross a kangaroo and a snake?
   A jump rope.

110. How do you know that carrots are good for your eyes?
   Have you ever seen a rabbit with glasses?

111. What do you call a rabbit with fleas?
   Bugs Bunny.

112. What do you call a penguin in the desert?
   Lost.

113. What kind of snack do little monkeys have with their milk?
   Chimps Ahoy!

114. When did the fly fly?
When the spider spied her!

115. What's gray on the inside and clear on the outside?
An elephant in a sandwich bag.

116. Where do worms like to go for dinner?
Anywhere that is dirt cheap.

117. Why do geese fly south for the winter?
Because they can't drive.

118. What do you get when you cross a porcupine and a turtle?
A slowpoke.

119. What kind of bird is like a car?

A goose—they both honk.

120. What do you call a baby goat when it is sleeping?

A kid-napping.

121. What animal makes it hard to carry on a conversation?

A goat, because he always wants to butt in.

122. A man rode into town on Monday, stayed five days, and then rode out on Monday. How is this possible?

His horse was named Monday.

123. What would you call a snake that drinks too much coffee?
A hyper viper.

124. What do you get when you cross a racehorse and french fries?
Fast food.

125. What do you call a nervous insect?
Jitterbug.

126. What school subject are snakes best at?
Hiss-tory.

127. What kind of money do marsupials use?
Pocket change.

128. What did the dachshund say when he won the race?
"I'm the wiener."

129. What can baby lizards do that baby snakes can't?
Learn to walk.

130. What do you call a group of mice in disguise?
A mouse-querade party.

131. Why did the kangaroo lose the basketball game?
He ran out of bounds.

132. What do ants get when they finish all their chores?
Allow-ants.

133. What's the best way to catch a squirrel?
    Climb a tree and act like a nut.

134. What do you call a bee that's having a bad hair day?
    A frizzbee.

135. How does a bird with a broken wing land safely?
    With its sparrowchute.

136. Why are frogs always happy?
    They eat whatever bugs them.

137. What snakes do babies like?
    Rattlesnakes.

138. What kind of bird is always sad?
A bluejay.

139. What do you get when you cross a potato with an elephant?
Mashed potatoes!

140. What kind of flowers would you give an absentminded squirrel?
Forget-me-nuts.

141. How do rabbits stay calm?
They say, "Don't worry, be hoppy."

142. Where do rabbits go right after their wedding?
On a bunnymoon.

143. What do you call a snail on a ship?
A snailor.

144. What is huge and gray and wears glass slippers?
Cinderellephant.

145. What do you do with a blue elephant?
Cheer him up!

146. What do you call a fly without wings?
A walk.

147. What do you call an infant insect?
A baby buggy.

148. What did the beaver say to the tree when he moved away?
"Nice gnawing you!"

149. What's a rabbit's favorite restaurant?
IHOP.

150. When is the best time to buy a pet bird?
When it's cheep.

151. How do little cubs keep their den cool in the summer?
With bear-conditioning.

152. How does a frog with no legs feel?
Unhoppy.

153. Why couldn't the snake talk?
He had a frog in his throat!

154. Why do bears have fur coats?
Because they look silly wearing sweaters.

155. What color socks do bears wear?
They don't wear socks; they have bear feet!

156. What's a penguin's favorite salad?
Iceberg lettuce.

157. How does a penguin make pancakes?
With its flippers.

158. What is a frog's favorite cold drink?
Croaka-Cola.

159. What is a frog's favorite hot drink?
Hot croako.

160. How does a penguin build its house?
Igloos it together.

161. What happened to the leopard that fell into the washing machine?
He came out spotless.

162. What is an owl's favorite school subject?
Owl-gebra.

163. Why did the bee go to the doctor?
Because it had hives.

164. What do you get when you cross a dinosaur with a pig?
Jurassic Pork.

165. What do you call two ants that run away to get married?
Antelopes.

166. What do you call an alligator detective?
An investigator.

167. What do you comb a rabbit with?
A harebrush.

168. How do you keep a skunk from smelling?
Hold its nose.

169. What did one firefly say to the other?
"You glow, girl!"

170. Why did the elephant paint himself different colors?
So he could hide in the crayon box.

171. How can you tell if an elephant has been in your refrigerator?
By the footprints in the butter.

172. What do you get when you cross a mouse with a squid?
An eek-topus!

173. What do frogs order at fast-food restaurants?
French flies.

174. What did the octopus say to his girlfriend when he proposed?
"Can I have your hand, hand, hand, hand, hand, hand, hand, hand in marriage?"

175. Where do killer whales go to hear music?
Orca-stras.

176. What do you call a cold dog sitting on a bunny?
A chili dog on a bun.

177. Where do mice park their boats?
At the hickory-dickory dock.

178. What do you call an alligator who steals all your stuff?
A crookodile.

179. What's an alligator's favorite drink?
Gatorade.

180. What do camels use to hide themselves?
Camelflauge.

181. What do you call a hippo that's a slob?
A hippopota-mess!

182. What is a lion's favorite state?
Maine.

183. What is a frog's favorite year?
Leap year.

184. Why are leopards so bad at hide-and-seek?
They're always spotted.

COMPUTERS AND CAREER COMEDY

· ·

185. Why did the college graduate go to work at the bank?
He heard there was money in it.

186. What snack do computer programmers like best?
Chips.

187. How did the computer criminal get out of jail?
He pressed the ESCAPE key.

188. Did you hear about the spider that enrolled in computer courses?
It wanted to learn web design.

189. What does the baby computer call its daddy?
Da-ta.

190. What's an astronaut's favorite part of a computer?
The space bar.

191. How did the tailor feel about his new job?
He thought it was sew-sew.

192. Why did the computer get up and leave the office?
To go have a byte of lunch.

193. How do you catch computer hackers?
With mousetraps.

194. What kind of computers wear shades?
    The ones that have Windows.

195. How are computers like soldiers?
    They all have to boot up.

196. Why was the butcher arrested?
    The police caught him chop-lifting.

197. Why did the queen go to the dentist?
    She wanted a new crown.

198. Why did the waitress lose her job?
    She refused to take orders from anyone.

199. Why do police officers need to be so strong?
So they can hold up traffic.

200. What do you call an archaeologist?
A scientist whose life is in ruins.

201. What do you call a person who doesn't return library books on time?
A bookkeeper.

202. What's another name for a dentist's office?
A filling station.

203. What do you call frozen police officers?
Copsicles.

204. What kind of nuts do bankers love best?
Cashews.

205. What's a lumberjack's favorite month?
Sep-tiiiimberrrrr!

206. What does a cowboy eat before a rodeo?
Bull-oney.

207. What is the favorite mode of transportation for accountants?
Taxis.

208. Why did the carpenter quit his job?
He was board.

209. What did the laptop do while it was at the beach?
It put on some screensaver and surfed the net.

210. Why don't computers eat anything?
They don't like what's on their menus.

211. How do you catch a run-away computer?
With an internet.

212. Which way did the programmer go?
He went data way.

213. Why shouldn't you take your computer into rush-hour traffic?
Because it might crash.

214. What case did the private investigator always doze off on?
The pillowcase.

215. How do cops greet new people?
"Policed to meet you."

216. Why didn't the fly go near the computer?
Because he was afraid he would get caught in the web.

217. What is the fastest way to annoy a doctor?
Take away his patients.

218. What kind of music do chiropractors listen to?
Hip-pop.

219. What does a cobbler say when a cat wanders into his shop?

"Shoe!"

220. What's an auto mechanic's favorite kind of candy?

Car-amels.

221. How do computers make sweaters?

With help from the inter-knit.

222. Why did the cat sit on the computer?

To keep an eye on the mouse.

223. What did the zookeeper like to eat for a snack?

Animal crackers.

224. What does a schoolteacher have in common with an eye doctor?

They both stare at pupils.

225. Why was the police officer under the blanket?

Because he was an under-cover cop.

226. What's a policeman's favorite way to fly?

In a heli-cop-tor.

227. Where should lazy people get jobs?

In bakeries, where they can loaf around.

228. What kind of clothes do lawyers wear?

Lawsuits.

229. What did the dentist of the year get at the awards ceremony?
A plaque.

230. What did the tooth say to the dentist as he left the room?
"Fill me in when you get back."

231. What did one tonsil say to the other?
"Dress up! The doctor is taking us out."

232. How do scientists cure their bad breath?
With experi-mints.

233. Why was the computer pro-grammer in so much back pain?
He slipped a disk.

234. What do hairstylists do when they're in a hurry?
Take shortcuts.

235. Why did the baker stop making donuts?
She was bored with the hole business.

236. Where do computers like to dance?
At the disk-o.

237. What did the judge say when the skunk walked into the courtroom?
"Odor in the court!"

238. What do dentists call their X-rays?
Tooth-pics.

239. Why did the computer go to the doctor?
It had a virus.

240. Why did the origami instructor quit her job?
It was too much paperwork.

241. What do postal workers do when they're angry?
They stamp their feet.

242. What nails do carpenters hate to hit?
Their fingernails.

243. Why did the news reporter go to the ice-cream parlor?
Because she wanted to get a good scoop.

244. What did the janitor say when he jumped out of the closet?

"SUPPLIES!"

FOOD FUNNIES

245. What kind of apple isn't an apple?
   A pineapple.

246. What's the difference between an Oreo cookie and a cheeseburger?
   Oreos taste much better dunked in milk.

247. How do you tell a chili pepper from a bell pepper?
   The chili pepper always wears a jacket.

248. Did you hear about the angry pancake?
   It just flipped.

249. Why did the M&M go to college?
 It wanted to be a Smartie.

250. How do you make an apple turnover?
 Roll it down a hill.

251. Why did the banana fail the driving test?
 It kept peeling out.

252. What do you call strawberries playing guitars?
 A jam session.

253. Where do hot dogs dance?
 At meatballs.

254. Jodi: "Would you like to join me in a cup of tea?"
Lilly: "I don't think we'd both fit."

255. How do you repair a broken casserole dish?
   With tomato paste.

256. What's the favorite food of Martians?
   Martian-mallows.

257. What do you call a pig thief?
   A hamburglar.

258. What kind of cookie makes you rich?
   A fortune cookie.

259. Why was the circus performer eating well-balanced meals?
He was training to be a tight-rope walker.

260. What do you call a kid who loves Chinese food?
A chow mein-iac.

261. What's black and shriveled up and giggles?
A ticklish raisin.

262. What do you call a lazy butcher?
A meat loafer.

263. Why was the birthday cake as hard as a rock?
It was marble.

264. Why doesn't bread like warm weather?

It gets too toasty.

265. What's a miner's favorite food?

Coal-slaw.

266. What did the apple say to the almond?

"You're nuts!"

267. Did you hear the one about the pizza?

Never mind, it's too cheesy.

268. When is a chef the meanest in the kitchen?

When he's beating the cake mix, mashing the potatoes, and whipping the cream.

269. What's a tree's favorite drink?
Root beer.

270. What's the best way for a guy to propose to a gal at a fast-food restaurant?
With an onion ring.

271. Who was the restaurant's star waiter?
Souperman.

272. What did the hamburger say to the pickle?
"You're dill-icious!"

273. How did the bubble gum cross the road?
On the bottom of the chicken's foot!

274. If Burger King married Dairy Queen, where would they live?
At White Castle.

275. What vegetable is a plumber's best friend?
A leek.

276. What has a fork and a mouth but never eats food?
A river.

277. Why did the man stare intently at the can of orange juice?
Because it said "concentrate."

278. What can't you eat for breakfast?
Lunch and dinner.

279. Did you hear the joke about the peach?
It was pitiful.

280. What do you call an apple with a short temper?
A crab apple.

281. What kind of cake is the favorite in heaven?
Angel food.

282. Why was the little cookie sad?
Because his mother was a wafer so long.

283. Why won't you ever find a lonely banana?
Because they always stay in bunches.

284. What kind of drink will give you a black-and-blue face?
   Punch.

285. What kind of coffee do you drink on the train?
   Expresso.

286. Why couldn't the coffee bean go out to play?
   It was grounded.

287. Why wasn't the girl hurt when she fell into a puddle of Pepsi?
   Because it was a soft drink.

288. What is the first sign that corn has a cold?
   It develops an earache.

289. What did the corn say when the farmer wanted to talk?
"I'm all ears."

290. Why did the Oreo go to the dentist?
It lost its filling.

291. Why did the other vegetables like the corn?
It was always willing to lend an ear.

292. Why was the ketchup last in the race?
It couldn't catch up.

293. What did the chef give his wife every morning?
A hug and a quiche.

294. What kind of nut comes without a shell?
   A donut.

295. What is most useful when it has been broken?
   An egg.

296. What's a pickle's favorite game show?
   Let's Make a Dill.

297. What did the cake say to the fork?
   "You want a piece of me?"

298. When do you go at red and stop at green?
   When you're eating a watermelon.

299. What did one coffee say to the other coffee?
   "Where you bean?"

300. What did the burrito say to the sad enchilada?
   "Do you want to taco 'bout it?"

301. What did the enchilada reply to the burrito?
   "It's nacho business."

302. Where do coffee lovers park their cars?
   In parking lattes.

303. What's the worst kind of jelly?
   Traffic jam.

304. What dance do pretzels do best?
   The twist.

305. How do you make a milk shake?
   Scare it!

306. How do you serve a smart hamburger?
   On an honor roll.

307. What's the best thing to put in a pie?
   Your teeth.

308. Why was the cucumber so mad?
   Because it was in a pickle.

309. What do you call a shoe that's made from a banana?
   A slipper.

310. What did the burger name her daughter?
   Patty.

311. What does toast wear to bed?
   Pa-jam-as.

312. What do hamburgers and long hair have in common?
   They both fit in a bun.

313. What's a millionaire's favorite dessert?
   Anything rich.

314. Why did the orange stop in the middle of the road?
It ran out of juice.

315. How do you make a rock float?
Put it in a glass with some ice cream and root beer.

316. What do you call the king of vegetables?
Elvis Parsley.

317. Why don't bananas ever snore?
They don't want to wake up the rest of the bunch.

318. What did one egg say to the other egg?
"Let's get crackin'!"

319. Why should you always bring a bag of chips to a party?
In queso emergency.

320. What's the scariest kind of noodle?
Spooketti.

321. Why do watermelons have big, fancy weddings?
Because they cantaloupe.

322. How do pickles enjoy a day out?
They relish it.

THE FUNNY FARM

323. Why did the cow enroll in drama class?
    To become a moo-vie star.

324. What's the favorite city of chickens?
    Chickago.

325. What tree is always unhappy?
    The blue spruce.

326. How was the horse able to pay for hay every day?
    He had a stable income.

327. What animal says "oom"?
    A backward cow.

328. What do you call a cow eating grass in your yard?
A lawn moo-er.

329. What do you hear when cows start singing?
Moo-sic.

330. What's the most common illness on a farm?
Hay fever.

331. What game do cows like to play?
Scrabbull.

332. Why can't you keep secrets on a farm?
Because the potatoes have eyes and the corn has ears.

333. Which is richer, a bull or a cow?

A bull. The cow gives you milk; the bull charges you.

334. What kind of chickens make everyone laugh?

Comedi-hens.

335. What do you call an Eskimo cow?

An Eski-moo.

336. What kept the performing pony from singing?

He was a little horse.

337. How do young chicks escape from their eggs?

Through the eggs-its.

338. Why did the chicken cross the playground?
   To get to the other slide.

339. Why did the rubber chicken cross the road?
   She wanted to stretch her legs.

340. What do you get when you cross a rooster and a bull?
   Roost beef.

341. How do you take a pig to the hospital?
   By hambulance.

342. What day of the week do chickens fear?
   Fry-day.

343. How do pigs say goodbye?
   With hogs and kisses.

344. Where do baby cows go for lunch?
   The calf-eteria.

345. What is a donkey's favorite game?
   Stable tennis.

346. What newspaper do cows read every morning?
   The Daily Moos.

347. What do chickens grow on?
   Eggplants.

348. Where did the sheep go for a haircut?

To the baa-baa shop.

349. In what direction do chickens always swim?

Cluckwise.

350. What do cows like to read best?

Cattle-logs.

351. What did the pig say at the beach on a hot summer's day?

"I'm bacon!"

352. What do chickens serve at birthday parties?

Coopcakes.

353. What's a lamb's favorite meat sauce?
Baa-baa-que sauce.

354. Why did the turkey cross the road?
It was the chicken's day off.

355. Why should you never tell a secret in a cornfield?
Because the stalks have ears.

356. Why did the cow go to the symphony?
He wanted to hear great moo-sic.

357. Why can't you be friends with a squirrel?
Because it will drive you nuts.

358. What do you get when you cross a pig with a teddy bear?
   A teddy boar.

359. Why did the pig go into the kitchen?
   He felt like bacon.

360. What do you call a bull taking a nap?
   A bulldozer.

361. What is a sheep's favorite pastime?
   Base-baa.

362. What do you tell a vegetable after it graduates from college?
   "Corn-gratulations!"

363. Where do pigs go to relax in the woods?
To their hog cabin.

364. What kind of trucks do pigs drive?
Eighteen-squealers.

365. What sweet treat do sheep like best?
Candy baas.

366. How did the farm team win the baseball game?
Their last little piggy ran all the way home.

367. Where do pigs get their money?
At the piggy bank.

368. What happens when a cow laughs too hard?

It cow-lapses.

369. What do you get if you feed gunpowder to a chicken?

An egg-splosion!

370. Where do you take sick ponies?

To the horse-pital.

371. Why didn't anyone laugh at the farmer's jokes?

They were too corny.

372. Why shouldn't you tell a secret to a pig?

He's a squealer.

373. What happens if pigs fly?
Bacon goes up.

374. What do pigs use to write letters?
Their pigpens.

375. What is a pig's favorite play?
Hamlet.

376. What do you get when you cross a pig and a tree?
A porky-pine.

377. What do you call a friendly horse who lives next door?
A nice neighhh-bor.

378. Lilly: "How is your new pig-powered car?"
Jodi: "It's okay except the tires squeal a lot."

379. What kind of horses only go out at night?
    Nightmares!

380. Why was the pig kicked off the soccer team?
    He hogged the ball.

381. What do you call a pig doing karate?
    A pork chop.

382. What is an owl's favorite mystery?
    A whoo-dunit.

383. What does the farmer talk about while he milks the cows?
Udder nonsense.

384. What do you call a grumpy cow?
Mooody.

385. What kind of thieves do you need to watch out for on the farm?
Pigpockets.

386. How did the owl with laryngitis feel?
He didn't give a hoot.

387. What dance are chickens afraid of?
The foxtrot.

388. What do detective ducks do?

Try to quack the case.

389. How can you tell if a pig is angry?

He goes hog wild.

390. What did the horse say when he fell down?

"I can't giddyup!"

391. Why did the cow jump over the moon?

He forgot where he left his rocket ship.

392. Where do sheep go on vacation?

To the Baa-hamas.

393. How do trees like to eat ice cream?

In pine cones.

394. How do you count a herd of cows?

With a cow-culator.

395. Where do cows go for fun?

To the moo-vies.

396. Where do injured rabbits go?

To the hop-spital.

397. Which tree is dressed the warmest?

A fir tree.

398. Where do worms prefer to shop?

In the Big Apple.

399. What do chickens do at Kentucky Fried Chicken?

They kick the bucket.

400. Why did the farmer spend the day stomping his field?

He wanted mashed potatoes.

401. Where do cows like to ride on the train?

In the cow-boose.

402. What did the farmer do at the chocolate factory?

Milk chocolates.

403. How do hogs get around the farm?

In pigup trucks.

404. Why did the farmer raise his children in a barn?

He wanted them to grow up in a stable environment.

405. Why is a barn so noisy?

All the cows have horns.

406. What happened to the turkey who got in a fight?

He got the stuffing knocked out of him.

407. Why do owls fly around at night?

It's faster than walking.

408. Where do ducks prefer to go on vacation?

The Duck-otas.

409. Why did the rock band hire a chicken?

They needed the drumsticks.

410. What kind of medicine do you give a sick horse?

Cough stirrup.

411. What did the tree say to his friend at the end of the day?

"I have to leaf."

412. What vegetable has the best rhythm?

A beet.

413. What do you get when you put five ducks in a box?
A box of quackers.

414. What role did the duck play in the animal orchestra?
He was the con-duck-tor.

415. What did the duck say when she bought lipstick?
"Put it on my bill."

416. What's a duck's favorite snack?
Cheese and quackers.

417. What's a farmer's favorite kind of car to drive?
A corn-vertible.

418. How did the farmer fix the holes in his jeans?
 With cabbage patches.

419. What time does a duck wake up?
 At the quack of dawn.

420. How do ducks celebrate the Fourth of July?
 They set off firequackers.

421. Did you hear the joke about the oak tree?
 It's acorny one.

422. Why was the pine tree grounded?
 For being knotty.

423. What do cows text one another?
  E-moo-jis.

424. How do chickens bake a cake?
  From scratch.

425. What does a mixed-up hen lay?
  Scrambled eggs.

426. What does an evil hen lay?
  Deviled eggs.

427. What do you get when a chicken lays an egg on top of a barn?
  An eggroll.

428. What is a scarecrow's favorite fruit?
Strawberries.

429. How do you keep a bull from charging?
You take away his credit card.

430. Why did the chicken cross the road, roll in mud, then cross the road again?
He was a dirty double crosser!

431. Why did the poultry farmer become a schoolteacher?
So he could grade his eggs.

432. What do you call an extra-round pumpkin?
A plumpkin.

433. Why do cows wear bells?
Because their horns don't work.

434. What do you call a cow that twitches?
Beef jerky.

435. Where do horses live?
In the neighhh-borhood.

436. What is a horse's favorite sport?
Stable tennis.

437. Why did the scarecrow win an award?
Because he was outstanding in his field.

HUMOR AT HOME

438. What kind of tree is only found in a house?

A pantry.

439. What did Sarah try to use to replace her lost tooth?

Toothpaste.

440. What never asks questions but gets a lot of answers?

A phone.

441. How do seven cousins divide five potatoes?

They mash them.

442. What's the tiniest room you'll ever find?

A mushroom.

443. What kind of parties do you have in the basement?

Cellar-brations.

444. What kind of party did the little girls throw for their dolls?

A summer Barbie-que.

445. Why do you put your photographs near the fireplace?

To make warm memories.

446. "Oooo! This wind is terrible," said Jodi. "It made a total mess of my hair."

"Yeah," agreed Lilly. "You look like you've been through a hair-icane."

447. What did Dad write on the bottom of his shoe?

A footnote.

448. Why didn't Mom pay the telephone bill?

She believed in free speech.

449. What happened when Dad saw the super-high electric bill?

He was shocked!

450. What goes up and down but doesn't move?
A staircase.

451. Who can jump higher than a house?
Anyone. A house can't jump.

452. What did one plate say to the other?
"Dinner is on me."

453. What runs but never gets anywhere?
A refrigerator.

454. Why did Dad sleep out in the garage, under the car?
He needed to wake up oily for an appointment.

455. What did one wall say to the other?

"Meet me in the corner."

456. What did the teddy bear say when he was offered dessert?

"No thanks, I'm stuffed."

457. Why did the boy tiptoe past the medicine cabinet?

He didn't want to wake the sleeping pills.

458. What did the first sock say to the second sock in the dryer?

"I'll see you the next time around."

459. What did the digital clock say to the grandfather clock?
"Look, Grandpa! No hands!"

460. What did Jodi and Lilly do when they found their dog, Jasper, eating the dictionary?
They took the words right out of his mouth.

461. What starts with *T*, ends with *T*, and is full of *T*?
Teapot.

462. What book has the most stirring topics?
A cookbook.

463. How much fun is doing laundry?
Loads!

464. Why can you always tell what Dick and Jane will do next?
They're so easy to read.

465. What did the mommy broom say to the baby broom?
"It is time to go to sweep."

466. What did the baby corn say to the mommy corn?
"Where is Pop-corn?"

467. Why did the house need to go to the doctor?
It had a window pain.

468. What do you get by putting ice in your father's bed?
A Popsicle.

469. Did you hear the joke about the roof?
Never mind, it's over your head.

470. What do you always find asleep in the dining room?
Napkins.

471. What did the mayonnaise say to the refrigerator?
"Close the door! I'm dressing."

472. Who stole soap from the bathtub?
The robber ducky.

473. Why was the broom late for school?
It overswept.

474. Why did the boy put candy under his pillow?
To have sweet dreams.

475. What is the scariest kind of laundry?
Boo-jeans.

476. What's big and gray and protects you from the rain?
An umbrella-phant.

477. What should you wear to Thanksgiving dinner?
A har-vest.

478. Why did the kid throw the butter out the window?
To see the butter fly.

479. What gives you the power and strength to walk through walls?

A door.

480. What did one toilet say to the other toilet?

"You look flushed!"

481. How do you warm up a room after it's been painted?

Give it a second coat.

482. What did the hat say to the scarf?

"You hang around, and I'll go ahead."

483. What do you call a guy lying on your doorstep?

Matt.

484. What did the lightbulb say to its mother?

"I wuv you watts and watts."

485. Why did the boy take a ruler to bed?

To see how long he slept.

486. Why was the boy sitting on his watch?

Because he wanted to be on time.

487. What did the little boy's mom say when he asked her to buy him shoes for gym?

"Tell Jim to buy his own shoes."

488. What did the clock do after it ate?

It went back four seconds.

489. Why did the TV cross the road?

Because it wanted to be a flat screen.

490. What do you get if you cross a fridge and a radio?

Cool music.

491. How do you scare someone out of the shower?

With sham-boo!

492. Why did the photograph go to prison?

Because it was framed.

493. What has one head, one foot, and four legs?

A bed.

494. What has two hands but no arms?

A clock.

JOKES ON THE MOVE

495. Why was the wheel the greatest thing ever invented?
It started everything rolling.

496. What travels faster, heat or cold?
Heat, because you can easily catch cold.

497. Why did the tire get fired from its job?
It couldn't stand the pressure.

498. Why can't car mufflers participate in marathon races?
They're too exhausted.

499. What is the only thing left after a train goes by?
 Its tracks.

500. What do you call a boxcar loaded with bubble gum?
 A chew-chew train.

501. What did the driver say when she came to a fork in the road?
 "This must be the place to eat."

502. What goes through towns and cities and up and over hills but never moves?
 A road.

503. What wiggles when it flies?
 A jellicopter.

504. Why do traffic lights turn red?
You would too if you had to change in the middle of the street!

505. Why won't you find much honey produced in Maryland?
There's only one *B* in Baltimore.

506. How do rabbits travel?
By hare-plane.

507. When is a bicycle not a bicycle?
When it turns into a driveway.

508. What did one elevator say to the other elevator?
"I think I'm coming down with something."

509. What happened to the wooden car with wooden wheels and a wooden engine?
It wooden go.

510. What is the best city to go bike riding in?
Wheeling, West Virginia.

511. What do you get when you buy a boat at a discount?
A sale boat.

512. What do you call a laughing motorcycle?
A Yamahahaha.

513. How did the boat show affection?
It hugged the shore.

514. What kind of dog watches NASCAR racing?
A lapdog.

515. What did the icy Arctic road say to the truck?
"Let's go for a spin!"

516. What did the traffic signal say to the truck?
"Don't look! I'm about to change."

517. What did the tornado say to the sports car?
"Let's go for a whirl!"

518. What part of a car is laziest?
The wheels, because they're always tired.

519. What kind of bagels can fly?
Plane ones.

520. How do trains hear?
With their engine-ears.

521. When is a car like a frog?
When it's being towed.

522. How do fleas travel?
By itch-hiking.

523. What has four wheels and flies?
A garbage truck.

524. What kind of snakes are for sale at the auto store?
Windshield vipers.

525. Who earns a living by driving their customers away?
A taxi driver.

526. Why doesn't a bike stand up by itself?
Because it's too tired.

527. What stays in the corner but travels far?
A stamp.

528. What driver doesn't need a license?
A screwdriver.

529. Where are cars most likely to get flat tires?
At forks in the road.

530. Why didn't the girl take the bus home?
Because her mom would make her take it back.

531. What do you call a scared train?
A fright train.

532. How does a train sneeze?
"Ah-choo-choo!"

533. Why did the boy throw a clock out the window?
To see time fly.

OUT OF THIS
WORLD JOKES

534. Why do people like jokes about rockets?
Because they're a blast.

535. What's the best way to have an adventure in space?
Plan-et.

536. Why did the alien get a ticket?
He forgot to pay the parking meteor.

537. Why will the sun always get the highest grades in school?
Because it is so bright.

538. What was the first animal in space?

The cow that jumped over the moon.

539. Why did Mickey Mouse go to outer space?

He was looking for Pluto.

540. What do you call a loony spaceman?

An astronut.

541. What do you call a tick on the moon?

A lunar-tick.

542. What is an astronaut's favorite meal?

Launch!

543. Why did the astronaut keep changing his course?
He didn't take the time to plan-et.

544. What is fast and loud and crunchy?
A rocket chip.

545. What holds the moon up?
Moonbeams.

546. What do you give an alien?
Space.

547. How do astronauts serve dinner?
On flying saucers.

548. What does the sun drink out of?
Sunglasses.

549. What do planets like to read?
Comet books.

550. How did the solar system hold up its pants?
With an asteroid belt.

551. Why did the people not like the restaurant on the moon?
Because there was no atmosphere.

552. When do astronauts eat their lunch?
At launchtime.

553. How does Santa deliver toys to aliens in outer space?
On U-F-Ho Ho Hos.

554. Where do astronauts keep their sandwiches?
In a launch box.

555. What did the astronaut think of the takeoff?
She thought it was a blast.

556. How do astronauts eat their ice cream?
In floats.

557. Why did the star get arrested?
Because it was a shooting star.

558. How does the Man in the Moon cut his hair?
Eclipse it.

559. Why didn't the sun go to college?
Because it already had a million degrees.

560. Why did the sun go to school?
To get brighter.

561. What did the alien say when he was out of room?
"I'm all spaced out!"

562. What kind of music do planets sing?
Neptunes.

563. What's a light-year?
The same as a regular year but with less calories.

564. Why did the cow go in the spaceship?
It wanted to see the mooon.

565. How do you know when the moon is going broke?
When it's down to its last quarter.

566. Why did the cow go to outer space?
To visit the Milky Way.

567. What did the doctor say to the rocket ship?
"Time to get your booster shot!"

568. Where are black holes usually found?
In black socks.

569. Why did the alien throw beef on the asteroid?
He wanted it a little meteor.

570. What should you do when you see a green alien?
Wait until it's ripe.

571. Why didn't the Dog Star laugh at the joke?
It was too Sirius.

572. What do you get when you cross a lamb and a rocket?
A space sheep.

573. What do you call a robot that always takes the longest route?
R2-Detour.

574. Why couldn't the astronaut book a room on the moon?
Because it was full.

575. What do aliens wear to weddings?
Space suits.

576. What do aliens love to drink?
Gravi-tea.

577. What do you say to a two-headed alien?
"Hello! Hello!"

578. What is an alien's favorite kind of social media?
Spacebook.

579. What do aliens like to roast over a fire?
Martian-mallows.

580. What do you call a skillet floating in outer space?
An unidentified frying object.

581. Why did the astronaut bring paper, scissors, and glue on his mission?
So he could do space-crafts.

582. Where do stars and planets go to school?
At the university.

583. What's the favorite food of astronauts?
Launch meat.

RAINING CATS
AND DOGS JOKES

584. What did the cat get on the test?
A purrr-fect score.

585. What do cats drink on hot summer afternoons?
Mice tea.

586. Where's the best place to park dogs?
In a barking lot.

587. What's a dog's favorite kind of bread?
Pupernickel.

588. How can you tell if a tree is a dogwood?

By its bark.

589. Where do editor dogs work?

At puplishing companies.

590. What was the dog doing in the mud puddle?

Making mutt pies.

591. What says, "Tick-tock-ruff-ruff"?

A watchdog.

592. How did the cat succeed in winning a starring role in a movie?

With purrr-sistence.

593. How do cats chill their drinks?

With mice cubes.

594. How did the dog get a nasty lump on his head?

It chased a parked car.

595. What should you name a dog who bites?

Gingersnap.

596. What city do small dogs love best?

New Yorkie.

597. What's the worst kind of cat to have?

A cat-astrophe.

598. What's a dog's favorite way to work out?
   Pupping iron.

599. What do you call a nature film about dogs?
   Dog-umentaries.

600. Who do dogs mail their Christmas wish lists to?
   Santa Paws.

601. Where do dogs wash their clothes?
   The laundro-mutt.

602. What do you call a dog who does magic tricks?
   A Labracadabrador.

603. Why did the cat family move next door to the mouse family?
So they could have the neighbors for dinner.

604. Where does a cat love to go on vacation?
Purrr-to Rico.

605. What do you call a lemon-eating cat?
Sourpuss.

606. What bone will a dog never eat?
A trombone.

607. How does a dog stop the movie he's watching?
He presses the PAWS button.

608. How do dogs get through rough times?

They keep very paw-sitive.

609. What wears a coat and pants all summer?

A dog.

610. What did the hungry Dalmatian say when he had a meal?

"That sure hit the spots."

611. Why did the collie dog marry the golden retriever?

He found her very fetching.

612. What do you call a dog with a cold?

A germy shepherd.

613. Where do little dogs sleep when they go camping?
In pup tents.

614. What do you call dogs who love to play in snow and ice?
Slush puppies.

615. Where do dogs like to go mountain climbing?
In Collie-rado.

616. What dog can jump higher than a tree?
All dogs. Trees don't jump.

617. What did the dog get when he multiplied 413 by 782?
The wrong answer.

618. What happens when you call a dog?

He comes to you.

619. What happens when you call a cat?

He takes a message.

620. What is noisier than a cat stuck in a tree?

Two cats stuck in a tree.

621. What do you call an overweight cat?

A flabby tabby.

622. What do you call a huge pile of kittens?

A meow-tain.

623. What did the cat on the smartphone say?

"Can you hear me meow?"

624. Why don't dogs like to travel on airplanes?

They get jet wag.

625. What is a cat's favorite breakfast cereal?

Mice Krispies.

626. How do you make a puppy disappear?

Use Spot remover.

627. Where are dogs afraid to shop?

At the flea market.

628. What do you call a puppy in January?
A chili dog.

629. What do you get when you cross Lassie with a petunia?
A collie-flower.

630. What kind of dog works for scientists?
A Lab.

631. What kind of carry-on did the puppy take on his trip?
A doggie bag.

632. What animal keeps the best time?
A watchdog.

633. What did the delegate from the UN name his dog?
Diplo-mutt.

634. What do you say when Fido eats your clock?
"That's alarming!"

635. Why did the dog sit in the shade?
He didn't want to be a hot dog.

636. What happened when Tommy's dog ate his watch?
The dog got lots of ticks.

637. What color do cats like best?
Purrr-ple.

638. How do you help a cat with a boo-boo?

With a first-aid kit.

639. Why are cats so good at video games?

They have nine lives.

640. What's a dog's favorite kind of pizza?

Pupperoni and cheese.

641. What's a cat's favorite game to play with a mouse?

Catch.

642. Where did the school cats go on a field trip?

To the mew-seum.

643. What's a cat's favorite song?

"Three Blind Mice."

644. Why are dogs like a phone?

They have collar IDs.

645. What did the dog say when he chewed on sandpaper?

"Ruff!"

646. What did the cowboy say when his dog was lost?

"Doggone it!"

647. What are caterpillars afraid of?

Doger-pillars.

648. What do you call a great dog detective?
Sherlock Bones.

649. What does a dog take for a tummyache?
Pupto Bismol.

650. What happens when it rains cats and dogs?
You might step in a poodle.

651. What happened to the dog who swallowed a firefly?
He barked with de-light.

652. What do you get when you cross a fly, a car, and a dog?
A flying car-pet.

653. What is totally funny and makes dogs itch?
The Flea Stooges.

654. What is a cat's favorite movie?
The Sound of Mew-sic!

655. What is the quietest kind of a dog?
A hush puppy.

656. What kind of cars do cats drive?
Cat-illacs.

SEASIDE KNEE-SLAPPERS

657. How do you join the fish choir?

You must be able to carry a tuna.

658. What is the most expensive fish?

A goldfish.

659. How much does a pirate pay to get his ears pierced?

A buck-an-ear.

660. What ocean animal is the most difficult to get along with?

The crab.

661. Who cleans house for fish and other sea creatures?
   Mermaids.

662. What do you call a surgeon with eight arms?
   A doc-topus.

663. What did the ocean say to the beach?
   Nothing. It just waved.

664. What did the scuba diver find shaking at the bottom of the bay?
   A nervous wreck.

665. In what country can fish survive out of water?
   Finland.

666. What's the most famous fish in the world?
The starfish.

667. What did the fishing boat captain say to the card magician?
"Pick a cod, any cod."

668. Who are hammerhead sharks' best friends?
Nailhead sharks.

669. What is a tropical fish's favorite food?
Reef-fried beans.

670. How do you catch a school of fish?
With a bookworm.

671. What can you always find to eat if you're shipwrecked on a deserted island?
Sand-wiches.

672. Where do fish sleep?
In waterbeds.

673. Who is always best dressed in the ocean?
The swordfish, who always looks sharp.

674. What fish smells the worst?
The stink-ray.

675. Why is an octopus so sweet?
It's covered in suckers.

676. What do sheep like to do in the ocean?
Scubaa dive.

677. Why did the fish go to jail?
The jury found him gill-ty.

678. What playground game do fish love best?
Salmon Says.

679. What happened to the man who put too many people on his boat?
He went a little overboard.

680. What kind of pizza will you find at the bottom of the ocean?
Deep-dish.

681. What do you get when you cross an octopus with a dog?
An octo-pooch.

682. What is messy, red, and has big claws?
A slob-ster.

683. When should you visit the Arctic Ocean?
When you just want to chill.

684. When does an ocean reef need a dentist?
When it has poor coral hygiene.

685. Where do sea cows sleep at night?
In barn-acles.

686. When do starfish go to the bathroom?
Whenever they have to twinkle.

687. What is an orca's favorite game show?
Whale of Fortune.

688. Why are fish afraid to play volleyball?
They might get caught in the net.

689. Where is the best place for fish to sleep?
In a riverbed.

690. What game do fish like playing the most?
Name That Tuna.

691. Why do fish like to travel in schools?
They like the group rates.

692. What animal is a weight-loss fanatic?
A fish. He carries his own scales around with him.

693. What animal is the best at fencing?
The swordfish.

694. What part of a fish weighs the most?
Its scales.

695. Why won't clams lend you money?
Because they are shellfish.

696. What kind of money do mermaids use?
Sand dollars.

697. What do you get when you cross an octopus with a pig?
An oink-topus.

698. What do you get when you cross an octopus with a parrot?
A squawk-topus.

699. What has a cat head but fish tail?
A purrr-maid.

700. What has two seats and sticks to ocean rocks?
A barnacle built for two.

701. How does a baby sponge learn about the ocean?
It lets it all soak in.

702. What did one shark say to the other while he ate a clownfish?
"This tastes funny."

703. What do you do with a boat that is sick?
Take it to the doc.

704. Why did the shark eat the tightrope walker?
He wanted a well-balanced meal.

705. What kind of hair do oceans have?
Wavy.

706. What is a shark's favorite game?
    Swallow the Leader.

707. Why does it take pirates so long to learn the alphabet?
    Because they spend a lot of years at C.

708. What is wrong with polluting the ocean?
    You make the sea sick.

709. Why are seagulls called seagulls?
    Because if they flew over the bay, they'd be bagels!

710. What do sea monsters eat for lunch?
    Fish and ships!

711. What do you get when you throw a million books into the ocean?
    A title wave.

712. Why do sharks live in salt water?
    Because pepper makes them sneeze.

713. What do fish take to stay healthy?
    Vitamin sea.

714. How do you make an octopus laugh?
    With ten-tickles.

715. How do you contact a fish?
    Drop him a line.

SILLY SCHOOL AND SPORTS JOKES

716. What kind of animal is always found at a baseball game?
A bat.

717. Why do golfers carry extra socks?
In case they get a hole in one.

718. Which baseball player is in charge of refreshments?
The pitcher.

719. What would you get if you crossed a baseball player with a frog?
An outfielder who catches flies and then eats them.

720. Why is baseball such a cool game?
Because of all the fans.

721. Why are frogs so good at basketball?
They always make jump shots.

722. What is the biggest diamond in the world?
A baseball diamond.

723. Why did the teacher jump in the pool?
She wanted to test the water.

724. How do you stay in contact with a baseball player?
You touch base every so often.

725. What is the best kind of shoe to wear for stealing bases?
  Sneakers.

726. Why do basketball players like to have cookies and milk for a snack?
  They like to dunk.

727. What did the bee teacher say to the naughty bee?
  "Bee-hive yourself!"

728. What kind of bee is always dropping the football?
  A fumble-bee.

729. When does royalty watch football?
  At knight games.

730. What do cheerleaders like to eat for breakfast?
Cheerios.

731. What kind of exercises are best for a swimmer?
Pool-ups.

732. What do history teachers talk about when they get together?
The old days.

733. What did one ball say to the other?
"See you 'round."

734. Why did the student eat his homework?
The teacher told him it was a piece of cake.

735. What do orthodontists do right before going on a roller coaster?

Brace themselves.

736. What brass instrument is twice as large as a tuba?

A fourba.

737. How do you clean your tuba?

With a tuba toothpaste.

738. What's a geologist's favorite kind of music?

Rock.

739. What did one math teacher say to the other?

"I've got a problem."

740. Where do numbers take a bath?

In mathtubs.

741. Why shouldn't you use a broken pencil?

Because it's pointless.

742. Why were the teacher's eyes crossed?

She couldn't control her pupils.

743. What's more difficult than cutting school?

Taping it back together.

744. Where do math teachers prefer to operate?

On multiplication tables.

745. Why was Mrs. Johnson's class abuzz?

It was having a spelling bee.

746. What happens when two ropes get into a contest?

They always tie.

747. What does a boxer like best about a good joke?

The punch line.

748. What does a cake have in common with a baseball game?

The batter.

749. Why do basketball courts get slippery?

The players dribble a lot.

750. How did the naughty class do on their bubble test?
They blew it.

751. What's a synonym?
A word you use when you can't spell the first one.

752. What do tennis players and waitresses have in common?
They both like to serve.

753. Which which teacher teacher always always uses uses words words twice twice?
A history teacher, because history always repeats itself.

754. What do you call a duck who plays basketball?
A slam duck.

755. Why did Cinderella get thrown off the baseball team?
Because she ran away from the ball.

756. What season do skydivers love the best?
Fall.

757. Where do you go to school to learn how to greet people?
Hi school.

758. Why did the teacher marry the school janitor?
Because he swept her off her feet!

759. What do English teachers eat for lunch?
Alphabet soup.

760. Why did the math teacher cry on the last day of school?
He hated being divided from his class.

761. Why did the teacher scold the student for something she didn't do?
She didn't do her homework.

762. Why did the football coach go to the bank?
To get the quarterback.

763. What is the best way to learn golf?
Take a course.

764. What is the best diet for a golfer?
Greens only.

765. Why did the teacher have to turn the lights on?

Because her class was so dim.

766. What is served but never eaten?

A tennis ball.

767. What do hungry golfers eat for lunch?

Their sand wedges.

768. Why was 6 afraid of 7?

Because 7, 8, 9.

769. What makes math such hard work?

All those numbers you have to carry.

770. How did the music teacher get into her classroom?
With a piano key.

771. Why did the equestrians get in trouble?
They wouldn't stop horsing around.

772. Why is tennis a noisy game?
Because when you play it, you have to raise a racket.

773. Why was there thunder and lightning in the chemistry lab?
Because the scientists were brainstorming.

774. Why did the mommy and daddy birds go to the school?
For a parrot-teacher conference.

775. What has forty feet and sings?
   The school choir.

776. Why did the star athlete never listen to music?
   She always broke the record.

777. Why did the choir kids climb ladders during rehearsal?
   So they could reach the high notes.

778. What did the baseball glove say to the baseball?
   "Catch you later!"

779. Why did the teacher wear sunglasses?
   Because her students were so bright!

780. Why did the kid study in the airplane?

He wanted a higher education.

781. Why did the cyclops stop teaching?

Because he only had one pupil.

782. What do you do if a teacher rolls her eyes at you?

Pick them up and roll them back to her.

783. Why did the teacher write on the window?

To make the lesson very clear.

784. Why wouldn't the man go rock climbing?

He wished he were boulder.

785. When is a baby good at basketball?
When it's dribbling.

786. What did one pencil say to the other?
"You're looking sharp!"

787. What do you call a slow skier?
A slope-poke.

788. What is a boxer's favorite drink?
Punch.

789. What is the world's longest punctuation mark?
The hundred-yard dash.

790. What school do you have to drop out of to graduate from?
Parachute school.

791. When is a baseball player like a spider?
When he catches a fly.

792. Why was the student's report card wet?
It was below C level.

793. Why can't you ever trust atoms?
They make up everything.

KNOCK YOUR SOCKS OFF
KNOCK-KNOCK JOKES

794. Knock knock.
   Who's there?
Ash.
   Ash who?
Bless you!

795. Knock knock.
   Who's there?
Howie.
   Howie who?
Howie gonna win the baseball game if you won't come out and play?

796. Knock knock.
   Who's there?
Tinker Bell.
   Tinker Bell who?
Tinker bell is out of order.

797. Knock knock.
   Who's there?
Abbey.
   Abbey who?
Abbey birthday to you!

798. Knock knock.
   Who's there?
Irish.
   Irish who?
Irish you would open the door.

799. Knock knock.
   Who's there?
Artichoke.
   Artichoke who?
Artichokes when he eats too fast.

800. Knock knock.
   Who's there?
Peas.
   Peas who?
Peas open the door and let me in.

801. Knock knock.
   Who's there?
Midas.
   Midas who?
Midas well let me in. I'm not going anywhere.

802. Knock knock.
   Who's there?
Arthur.
   Arthur who?
Arthur any mean dogs around here?

803. Knock knock.
   Who's there?
Owl.
   Owl who?
Owl tell you if you promise not to reveal my owl-dentity.

804. Knock knock.
　Who's there?
Watson.
　Watson who?
Watson the grill? I'm hungry.

805. Knock knock.
　Who's there?
Atlas.
　Atlas who?
Atlas, it's the weekend!

806. Knock knock.
　Who's there?
Lettuce.
　Lettuce who?
Lettuce in! It's raining out here!

807. Knock knock.
　Who's there?
Osborn.
　Osborn who?
Osborn on this day! It's my birthday!

808. Knock knock.
   Who's there?
Jilly.
   Jilly who?
**It's Jilly out here, so open
the door!**

809. Knock knock.
   Who's there?
Ken.
   Ken who?
**Ken you come out and play this
afternoon?**

810. Knock knock.
   Who's there?
Theodore.
   Theodore who?
**Theodore is shut. Can you open
it, please?**

811. Knock knock.
   Who's there?
Turnip.
   Turnip who?
Turnip the stereo, please.

812. Knock knock.
   Who's there?
Police.
   Police who?
Police open the door.

813. Knock knock.
   Who's there?
Kenya.
   Kenya who?
Kenya gimme a dollar to buy an ice-cream cone?

814. Knock knock.
   Who's there?
Jess.
   Jess who?
Jess open the door and don't ask questions.

815. Knock knock.
Who's there?
Anita.
Anita who?
Anita flashlight so I can see in the dark.

816. Knock knock.
Who's there?
Sandy.
Sandy who?
Sandy door, please. I just got a splinter.

817. Knock knock.
Who's there?
Bean.
Bean who?
Bean fishing lately?

818. Knock knock.
Who's there?
Avocado.
Avocado who?
Avocado cold.

819. Knock knock.
   Who's there?
Alaska.
   Alaska who?
Alaska your dad if you can come out to play.

820. Knock knock.
   Who's there?
Stan.
   Stan who?
Stan back. I'm coming in.

821. Knock knock.
   Who's there?
Eddie.
   Eddie who?
Eddiebody who comes too close to me might catch my cold.

822. Knock knock.
   Who's there?
Annie.
   Annie who?
Annie time you're ready, come out and play. We're waiting on you.

823. Knock knock.
   Who's there?
Europe.
   Europe who?
Europe mighty early this morning.

824. Knock knock.
   Who's there?
Atch.
   Atch who?
Sounds like you have a cold.

825. Knock knock.
   Who's there?
Water.
   Water who?
Water you doing later tonight?

826. Knock knock.
   Who's there?
Avenue.
   Avenue who?
Avenue heard this knock-knock joke before?

827. Knock knock.
   Who's there?
Juno.
   Juno who?
Juno what time it is?

828. Knock knock.
   Who's there?
Warrior.
   Warrior who?
Warrior been? I've been knocking for hours!

829. Knock knock.
   Who's there?
Dishes.
   Dishes who?
Dishes me. Who are you?

830. Knock knock.
   Who's there?
Dismay.
   Dismay who?
Dismay seem funny, but I'm not laughing!

831. Knock knock.
   Who's there?
Icon.
   Icon who?
Icon tell you another one of these knock-knock jokes.

832. Knock knock.
   Who's there?
Gruesome.
   Gruesome who?
Gruesome tomatoes in my garden.

833. Knock knock.
   Who's there?
Nobel.
   Nobel who?
Nobel, so I knocked.

834. Knock knock.
   Who's there?
Isaiah.
   Isaiah who?
Isaiah again, "Knock knock."

835. Knock knock.
   Who's there?
Butter.
   Butter who?
Butter let me in!

836. Knock knock.
  Who's there?
Tank.
  Tank who?
You're welcome.

837. Knock knock.
  Who's there?
D-1.
  D-1 who?
D-1 who knocked!

838. Knock knock.
  Who's there?
Ears.
  Ears who?
**Ears another knock-knock joke
for you.**

839. Knock knock.
  Who's there?
Repeat.
  Repeat who?
Who. Who. Who!

840. Knock knock.
   Who's there?
Omelet.
   Omelet who?
Omelet smarter than I look!

841. Knock knock.
   Who's there?
Orange.
   Orange who?
Orange you going to open the door?

842. Knock knock.
   Who's there?
Lettuce.
   Lettuce who?
Lettuce use your phone, please!

843. Knock knock.
   Who's there?
Pizza.
   Pizza who?
Pizza really great guy!

844. Knock knock.
　Who's there?
Cargo.
　Cargo who?
Cargo *beep beep*.

845. Knock knock.
　Who's there?
Dougnut.
　Donut who?
Donut ask, it's a secret!

846. Knock knock.
　Who's there?
Doris.
　Doris who?
Doris locked, that's why I knocked.

847. Knock knock.
   Who's there?
Dewey.
   Dewey who?
Dewey have to keep telling silly jokes?

848. Knock knock.
   Who's there?
Anita.
   Anita who?
Anita drink of water, please!

849. Knock knock.
   Who's there?
Ice-cream soda.
   Ice-cream soda who?
Ice-cream soda whole world will know you won't let me in!

850. Knock knock.
Who's there?
Stopwatch.
Stopwatch who?
Stopwatch you're doing and open this door!

851. Knock knock.
Who's there?
Luke.
Luke who?
Luke through the peephole and you'll see.

852. Knock knock.
Who's there?
Alex.
Alex who?
Alex the questions around here.

853. Knock knock.
   Who's there?
Sadie.
   Sadie who?
Sadie magic word and I'll disappear.

854. Knock knock.
   Who's there?
Mikey.
   Mikey who?
Mikey doesn't fit in the keyhole. Let me in!

855. Knock knock.
   Who's there?
Dozen.
   Dozen who?
Dozen anyone want to let me in?

856. Knock knock.
   Who's there?
Iowa.
   Iowa who?
Iowa friend a couple dollars.

857. Knock knock.
   Who's there?
Deena.
   Deena who?
Deena you hear me the first time?

858. Knock knock.
   Who's there?
Roach.
   Roach who?
Roach you a letter. Didn't you get it?

859. Knock knock.
  Who's there?
Samoa.
  Samoa who?
Samoa ice kweam, pwease.

860. Knock knock.
  Who's there?
Dune.
  Dune who?
Dune anything fun this afternoon?

861. Knock knock.
  Who's there?
Phillip.
  Phillip who?
Phillip the dog's water bowl, please. He's very thirsty.

862. Knock knock.
  Who's there?
Cozy.
  Cozy who?
Cozy who's knocking!

863. Knock knock.
   Who's there?
Snow.
   Snow who?
Snowbody!

864. Knock knock.
   Who's there?
Juno.
   Juno who?
Juno how to open this door? It's stuck!

865. Knock knock.
   Who's there?
Ivana.
   Ivana who?
Ivana come in. Will you open the door?

866. Knock knock.
   Who's there?
Howard.
   Howard who?
Howard I know?

867. Knock knock.
   Who's there?
Wooden shoe.
   Wooden shoe who?
Wooden shoe like to open the door and find out?

868. Will you remember me in one minute?
   Yes.
Knock knock.
   Who's there?
Hey! You didn't remember me!

A HODGEPODGE
OF HUMOR

869. What do you call pictures of your feet?
Foot-ographs.

870. What clothing does a house wear?
Address.

871. What can you break just by calling its name?
Silence.

872. Who loves to solve mysteries and soak in bubble baths?
Sherlock Foams.

873. What do you call Batman after he's been run over by a steamroller?
Flatman.

874. Why are snowmen so popular?
They're just so cool!

875. Who steals from the rich, gives to the poor, and carries a picnic basket?
Little Red Robin Hood.

876. Can February March?
No, but April May.

877. What's an infant's favorite plant?
Baby's breath.

878. What can you catch but not hold?
   A cold.

879. What kind of language do billboards use?
   Sign language.

880. What gets lost every time you stand up?
   Your lap.

881. What kind of tree has the best bark?
   A dogwood.

882. How do angels greet one another?
   "Halo!"

883. What bites without any teeth?
   Frost.

884. What do people make that you can't see?
   Noise.

885. What is the one thing you can always count on?
   Your fingers.

886. Why did the tree go to the dentist?
   It needed a root canal.

887. What kind of pet makes the loudest noise?
   A trum-pet.

888. What do you give a mummy for Christmas?
Wrapping paper.

889. What do snowmen have for breakfast?
Frosted Flakes.

890. What does a tree do when it is ready to go home?
It leaves.

891. What do soldiers hate most?
The month of March.

892. Why did Batman stop at the pet store?
He was looking for a Robin.

893. What part of your body has the most rhythm?
Your eardrums.

894. Where do walnuts look for their brothers and sisters?
In the family tree.

895. What's the best thing to take on a trip to the desert?
A thirst-aid kit.

896. When rain falls, does it ever go up again?
Yes, in dew time.

897. What do you get if you cross Father Christmas with a detective?
Santa Clues.

898. If Santa rode a motorcycle, what kind would it be?
A Holly-Davidson.

899. Which of Santa's reindeer has bad manners?
Rude-olph.

900. What do Santa's beard and a Christmas tree have in common?
They both need trimming.

901. What do elves learn in school?
The elf-abet.

902. What is Santa's favorite outdoor activity?
Gardening. He loves to ho, ho, ho.

903. What bus sailed across the Atlantic Ocean?
Columbus.

904. Which vegetable wasn't allowed on Columbus's ships?
The leek.

905. What is in a ghost's nose?
Boo-gers.

906. Why was the computer so tired when it got home from the office?
Because it had a hard drive.

907. What is a good name for a thief?
Rob.

908. What do snowmen wear on their heads?

Ice caps.

909. What do you call a sleeping dinosaur?

A bronto-snore-us.

910. What kind of case does a detective always crack?

A nutcase.

911. What's another name for a sleeping dinosaur?

A sleep-asaurus.

912. What do snowmen eat for lunch?

Icebergers.

913. What do you call a dinosaur cowboy?
Tyrannosaurus Tex.

914. What do you call a dinosaur that sings?
A rock-osaurus.

915. What are prehistoric reptiles called when they sleep?
Dino-snores.

916. Why wasn't Cinderella good at sports?
Because she had a pumpkin as her coach.

917. What did the Gingerbread Man use to fasten his vest?
Gingersnaps.

918. Where does a ghost go on vacation?
Maliboo.

919. What did Cinderella say while she was waiting for her photos?
"Someday my prints will come."

920. How did the Gingerbread Man make his bed?
With cookie sheets.

921. Why was Snow White elected to the Supreme Court?
She was the fairest of them all.

922. What kind of flower grows on your face?
Tulips.

923. What did the flower say to the bee?
"Quit bugging me!"

924. Why did Santa's elves go to music school?
To improve their rapping skills.

925. Why is Alabama the smartest state in the United States?
Because it has four As and one B.

926. What is the best state to buy a small bottle of cola in?
Minisoda.

927. Where can you find roads without cars, forests without trees, and cities without houses?
On a map.

928. What goes from Maine to Florida without moving?
The highway.

929. What state is the cleanest?
Washington.

930. What is the most slippery country in the world?
Greece.

931. What country gets all stirred up?
Mix-ico.

932. Where was the Declaration of Independence signed?
On the bottom.

933. What did the boy volcano say to the girl volcano?

"I lava you!"

934. When does Friday come before Thursday?

In the dictionary.

935. If April showers bring May flowers, what do May flowers bring?

Pilgrims.

936. How were George Washington's wigs delivered?

By hair-mail.

937. Why does the Statue of Liberty stand in New York Harbor?

Because she can't sit down.

938. What did Paul Revere say at the end of his famous ride?
"Whoa!"

939. What was the colonist's favorite drink?
Liber-tea.

940. Why did the skeleton go to the party alone?
It had no body to go with.

941. Where on Noah's ark did the bees stay?
In the ark-hives.

942. What kind of lights did Noah put on the ark?
Floodlights.

943. What did Noah do for a living?

He was an ark-itect.

944. What animals spent most of the time on their knees while on the ark?

Birds of prey.

945. What did Noah say to the toads?

"Wart's new?"

946. What did Noah say to the frogs?

"Hop on in!"

947. Did the worms on Noah's ark live inside apples?

No, they had to be in pairs.

948. Why didn't Jonah trust the ocean?
There was something fishy about it.

949. Why didn't Noah's sons play cards on the ark?
Because their dad was standing on the deck.

950. Which animals were hardest for Noah to trust?
The cheetahs.

951. What belongs to you but other people use more often?
Your name.

952. What kind of bow is impossible to tie?
A rainbow.

953. What was Boaz like before he got married?
Ruthless.

954. Who was the fastest runner in history?
Adam. He was first in the human race.

955. Who is the greatest babysitter mentioned in the Bible?
David. He rocked Goliath to a very deep sleep.

956. What kind of roof is always wet?
The roof of your mouth.

957. What's easy to get into but hard to get out of?
Trouble.

958. How do trees get on the internet?
They log in.

959. What did the snowman say to the customer?
"Have an ice day!"

960. What is a tornado's favorite game to play?
Twister.

961. What do you have in December that you don't have in any other month?
The letter *D*.

962. Why is a skeleton so mean?
It doesn't have a heart.

963. Which animal had the highest level of intelligence on Noah's ark?
The giraffe.

964. What kind of dinosaur had the best vocabulary?
The thesaurus.

965. Where do snowmen go to dance?
To a snowball.

966. What can you hold without touching it?
Your breath.

967. How many animals did Moses take on the ark?
Moses didn't take any animals on the ark. Noah did.

968. Why didn't Noah fish very often?

He only had two worms.

969. Why are mountains so funny?

Because they are hill-areas.

970. What kind of music do balloons hate?

Pop.

971. How did the telephone propose to its girlfriend?

It gave her a ring.

972. Why is Hawaii such a favorite vacation spot?

It's so lava-ble.

973. Why can't your nose be twelve inches long?
Because that would be a foot!

974. Why did the thief shower right before he robbed the bank?
To make a clean getaway.

975. What did the stamp say to the envelope?
"Stick with me and we'll go far."

976. What did the dinosaur say after his workout?
"I'm so sore-us!"

977. Did you hear about the paperboy?
He blew away.

978. What US state does the most laundry?
Washington.

979. What does a cloud wear under its raincoat?
Thunderwear.

980. What rock group has four guys who don't sing?
Mount Rushmore.

981. What building has the most stories?
The library.

982. What state is always happy?
Merry-land.

983. Why did the boy have his girlfriend put in jail?
She stole his heart.

984. Where do crayons go on vacation?
   Color-ado.

985. Why should you never tell a joke while standing on ice?
   Because it might crack up.

986. How do Eskimos make their beds?
   With sheets of ice and blankets of snow.

987. Why was the robot mad?
   People kept pushing its buttons.

988. Why don't mountains get cold in the winter?
   They wear snowcaps.

989. What do you call a snow-man in the desert?
A puddle.

990. What did one eye say to the other?
"Between you and me, something smells."

991. What do you call a king who is only twelve inches tall?
A ruler.

992. What did the one penny say to the other penny?
"We make perfect cents."

993. What can you put in a barrel to make it lighter?
Holes.

994. What did one hair say to the other?

"It takes two to tangle!"

995. What did one bucket say to the other?

"I am feeling pail today."

996. What do you call a fairy who doesn't take a bath?

Stinker Bell.

997. What's the best parting gift?

A comb.

998. What would you call a humorous knee?

Fun-knee.

999. Why did the teddy bear need a doctor appointment?
He was all stuffed up.

ABOUT THE EDITORS

Jodi and Lilly Simmons are sisters who live in Ohio with their parents and two funny dogs named Jasper and Daisy, who are hilarious when they play tug-of-war. Jodi is ten years old and likes the beach, art, dancing, swimming, and reading. Lilly is eight years old and likes music, dolls, dancing, and making new friends. They both love to be silly and laugh, so they wanted to make this book as funny as possible. Jodi and Lilly also helped their mom write a devotional book called *How God Grows a Girl of Grace*.

Continue the Fun With...

999 Super Fun, Head-Scratching, Brain-Boosting Bible Trivia Questions for Kids

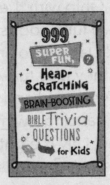

Kids love to learn about the Bible—and here's a fantastic collection of 999 Bible trivia questions especially for 6- to 12-year-olds! Compiled and edited *by* kids *for* kids, you can be sure this is a collection of trivia that young readers will enjoy and share—with anyone who will listen!

Paperback / 978-1-68322-560-7 / $4.99